love me

Virginia Little

Published by Salt Water Media
29 Broad Street, Suite 104
Berlin, MD 21811
www.saltwatermedia.com

Salt Water
MEDIA

Cover image by Paulina Hammond

how do i release something
that is truly 100% me
do i want my whole heart out there
for people to see and give their
judgement about?
can i take that?
do i want to make all of my private
business public?
do i want to let everyone in
like my heart and soul is a
welcome mat?
i guess we'll find out

missed call (4) ****

stardust
were all made out of stardust
while spending my last day as stardust
i wanted to spend it with
your stardust
the one person i didnt have to run from
i didnt have to hide
i let you in
and thats not easy for me to do
the walls were caving in
and yet
right before they did
your stardust saved me
it lead me to get help
it lead me to you
so thank you stars
for using your dust
and making her.

i look into a flame
a flame ive created
i stare for too long
and the flame blends together
all i see is light
i see all the things we used to be
you were my light at one point in time
i blow the flame out
too many painful memories
i stared at the light too long
now whenever i blink
i just see you

i am my own soulmate
what are the chances that my brain
would be put in my body
there are so many possibilities
that i know
i was made for myself

the thought of being able to
write about anything scares me

i could write about love
i could write about loss
i could write about lust
i could write about life
i could write about death
i could write about losing my mom
in the grocery store
i could write about losing my mom
in general
i could write about walking through my
grandads house for the first time in
ten years
i could write about my childhood

i have so much power within my
fingertips and within my words

im just scared about
whether or not
the softness of my soul comes across
or the hardness of my hands

sometimes crying is the best medicine

WITH HANDS AS SOFT AS BED SHEETS
AND LIPS AS SMOOTH AS MARBLE

I AM CONSUMED BY YOUR BEAUTY

you held my heart in your hands
something so soft and delicate

instead of taking care of it
and cherishing it

you gripped tight
and watched it bleed

with no words
with just the look
of an eye
i know that i am yours
and you are mine

when you have lost youre way
and have nowhere to go

find that moment where you first got
lost
live in it all over again
and choose a different path then the
one
you took

you always say what
youd be without me
how lonely youd be
how much you would miss me

but you never seem to think
about what id be without you

id be nothing
youve taught me so much
about myself
things i didnt know but you saw them

without you i am a shell
of who i am

my life is a book
and while im honored to have
you as a chapter in it

im so glad its over

you have to let the pain in
you have to bathe in it

you cant run from it forever

you have to feel
everything
if you ever want to feel
anything

our souls are

reaching for each other
like
feet reaching for
a cold spot in bed

shes like art

you can look but
you cant touch

fall in love with someone
for their eyes
looks will fade
but the eyes never change

you can fall out of love
but you can never stop
caring about that person

you prick me like
a cactus pricks fingers

your name used to bring me
so much joy
now when i hear it
i cringe
i get a bitter taste in my mouth
i remember when it used to bring
me so much joy
and now all it brings is pain

moving on is not avoiding someone that
you loved
but learning how to live with them in
your life

there is a dark place inside
of my head
i hate to go there but sometimes
i cant help it

it consumes me
it eats me whole
i am left a shell of a person
a person that does things that
i am not proud of

i learn to live with this dark places
but not in it
i learn to find the light place and
run to it as fast as i can

sometimes i fail and go back to the
dark place
i live in it and let it control me
but then i see the light place
with the door cracked just a little
and run to it as fast as i can

looking at you is like
looking at myself
i see what i have become from you
and i dont know
if i love it
or hate it

flowers cant grow without sunshine
and neither can you

i fell in love with
you not when i layed
eyes upon you but
when my soul layed
eyes upon yours

death is what
gives life purpose

i felt you scars
my fingers tracing the small
lines where you let yourself bleed
when you saw me feeling the pain
you once felt
i saw the hurt behind your eyes
and its something i never want to see
again
and in that moment all i could think
was
why was i not there?

i give you everything
all that i have
yet it is still not enough

for you are everything i have
and so much more

no matter how you love
you love weirdly
people that hide it are weird because
love can so simply be shown
in the look of an eye

people that shout it from
the rooftops
are weird because
who does that?

no matter how you love someone
it is completely unique
and completely beautiful

i dont know if we will
stay closer than ever
or
if well see each other
in the grocery store and act
like we never knew each other
or
if well be those old friends
that when they get back together
its like they were never apart

sunrise
we sit on the roof
and dream that we are the sun
we want to be apart of something
so beautiful and something so important
that we cant survive without it
little did you know
you are my sun

when someone admires my work
it is the best feeling
because
they are admiring the real
me

no matter how much you think
that you hate me
i will always have the power
to make you laugh

i watch you sleep
i watch your chest rise and fall
you steal the covers but i dont care
as long as you are warm
i am warm too
when you wake
i wont be there

be who you want to be
no one else will have to live in your
mind
no one is trapped in your soul
no one has your heart
character
or spirit

so be you
because no one else out there is you
and the world needs someone like you

who ever said words
dont hurt
is the biggest liar
because physical pain goes away
but emotional pain stays
it finds a place in your mind and heart
and makes a home out of it

i am not scared of death
it will happen to me
to all of us
what i am scared of is
that when i die
i will not be ready
and wont have accomplished
everything that i wanted to

the weirdest thing ive ever felt
was when you were talking to me
and smiling
and i looked in your eyes
and got lost
the world literally stopped
and all i could think was
how lucky i was to be alive at the same
time as you
and that i got to know you
and that maybe
just maybe
you felt the same

im not sure
if you stress me out more
than you make me happy
its a very fine line

pink is your favorite color
mine too
we both like a light pink
not the dark
reminds us of hope
and the stars

were so similar
souls alike
hearts apart

now when i see light pink
i think of you
not my favorite color
but yours too

i saw you so close to slipping through
my fingertips
and all i could think was

please dont leave me
please dont leave me
please dont leave me
please dont leave me
please dont leave me
please dont leave me
please dont leave me
please dont leave me
please dont leave me
please dont leave me
please dont leave me
please dont leave me
please dont leave me
please dont leave me
please dont leave me
please dont leave me
please dont leave me
please dont leave me
please dont leave me
please dont leave me
please dont leave me
please dont leave me
please dont leave me
please dont leave me
please dont leave me
please dont leave me
please dont leave me
please dont leave me
please dont leave me
please dont leave me
please dont leave me

there are so many thoughts
that cross your mind
that you never say out loud

you think of so many words
that are left unsaid

i wish i could somehow
pick your brain
and hear all of those thoughts

people have so many ideas
of who you are and
who youre supposed to be

i see right through all those
common misconceptions

i see theres another world
behind your eyes
i see a light shining from within
that maybe others cant see

just talk to me
what are you running from?

why do you always call me when you
need something other than me

i dont care if you hook up with random
people
i dont care if you kiss someone else
i dont care that you dont kiss me
i care about if you are kissing someone
that
loves you and cares about you like i do
and when you do dumb things
and hook up with people that dont care
about you
and kiss people for the hell of it
it hurts
because i give you my everything
and yet i am still not good enough for
you

ive always thought that
i would have to save you
that you were the broken one
i didnt know that
on the inside
i was the one that needed to be saved

if i could
i would feel nothing
yet
that scares me

you only care
when its convenient
for you

i may be able to wash your
DNA from my skin
but i will never be able to
wash your imprint off

with such a warm face
you had such a cold heart

when i look back on happy memories
i always smile
but have tears in my eyes
because what if ive peaked
what if ill never feel that good again
what if the good times are already past
me
and i cant go back to them
no matter how fast i run

first loves will teach you so much
about yourself
things you will never truly
understand till you love someone
romantically for the first time
you will fall harder than ever
and think that there is no getting back
up
but there will be a second love
that will be just as great
or better

because i believe we met each other for
a reason. there are 7 billion people in
the world and im lucky enough to call
you my friend. we should keep it that
way

when you fall in love
with a person
you study them
you watch all their small moves
you listen to every word they say
you pay attention to the small details
you notice bad habits
and what they like
and dont like
you can tell when they are stressed
or sick
or when anything is slightly off
you know
you just know

i am empty
i am hollow
i have become a shell
i have skin
and bones
and a brain
and a heart
but i am still nothing
i am a waste
no one cares
no one loves
no one trusts

-3 am thoughts

a piece of me
will always be yours
there will be certain times
and certain places
where you will pop in my mind
and i will remember you
a long time period of my life
was dedicated to you
you have a chapter in my book
and i dont mind
because you are apart of me
and my story
i wont forget you
because you are just as much me
as i am

i want to tell you how
i really feel
i want to cuss you out like
theres no tomorrow
but im so afraid of losing you that
i bite my tongue
and repress my feelings
when maybe i shouldnt

i care too much
about people who
would hurt me
and then when i tell them
that they hurt me
they try to argue
whether or not i should be hurt

you look so deep into my soul
that you find things
that even i didnt know
were ever there

walking through the lonely london
streets
feeling the rain drip down my smooth
skin

i realized i belong in no one specific
place

i am in a world that deserves my pres-
ence

a world that needs to be discovered
by my eyes

there are too many beautiful places
that i need to look upon

i need to chase the sun
i need to fly above the mountains
swim and soak in the seas

i need to go everywhere i can

i have a burning desire to see and be
everything
there is possible

i will find myself in the setting sun
and rising moon

i will go
where
my heart takes me

you control my mind
i try to sleep but i cant

my thoughts are taken over by your body
my hands burn to touch your skin

i want to use all my senses with you
come alive

will you let me?

we are the universe
we are stars
and air
and so many beautiful things

we are love
we are darkness
and sunshine

we make up every component
of ourselves
every fiber
DNA
atoms

we are it
we are the sun
and the mood
we make them shine
for us
for light in the darkness
and brightness in the best of times

we are anything that we want to be

our love can never die
as long as
you remember me
and i remember you
we will always carry a piece
of each other

i may not love you anymore
but i will always want the best for you
ive always just wanted you to be happy
with or without you

i wish you could see
yourself
like i see you
you would finally realize
how much impact you truly have

i have so many
people that care about me
we all do
we just forget it sometimes

i write these words
for myself
and only myself
to help heal
and get it out
i release my work to
heal others

we sit looking at the stars
i feel your cold body wrap around mine
i want to be your heat
i want to be your star

as we sit there
i am the most calm ive ever been
you
the stars
its all overwhelming
my fingers trace circles on you hands
my lips pressed against yours
i feel your heat
i am your star

i think to myself
does life get better than this?
i dont know if it does or not
but if it does
i cant wait to get there

i miss you

no, you arent dead
no, we are still friends

i miss the way things were
in a world so cold
you were the fire to melt the ice

now youre nothing but a burnt out match

i choke on my words
as i taste them on my tongue
you always do this to me

what do i say
how do i say it
with something so perfect in front of
me
how do i not break it

i touch you so softly
run my fingertips across your skin
lips parted like a waterfall
eyes wide staring at a masterpiece

i care
i care more than youll
ever know

i just cant show it

i held your hand
yet i felt empty handed

do you talk to her about me
do you tell her about
all weve been through
the moments
the stories
what weve shared
the thoughts that crossed
our minds

maybe you have
maybe you havent
either way
i know you still think about it

i used to beg for your attention
and you would never give it

now i dont crave
and you give it anyways

funny how time works

i have found my paradise
no it is not with someone
but with myself
you need to find yourself
before you can find anything else

when my soul was not at rest
and i tried to look for things
i often found dark places inside myself
that i never want to find again

but in these dark places
i found the light
i found myself
and i wouldnt have it any other way

i took my pain
and made art

writing poetry comes out of
the deepest pain you could ever feel
the deepest cuts

i thought that i was writing it out of
hate

hate for myself
hate for the world
hate for the people around me

looking back i realize
it was just me

it was my doubts
and insecurities

i left a piece of myself on these pages
each one is like a little drop of my
DNA

through writing all this
i found myself
i found who i want to be
i found happiness

everyday i try to improve and become
more
and more of myself

believe me
not everyday is gonna be the best
but youll get there

learn from me
my writings
my words
as you have experienced it here on
these pages

www.ingramcontent.com/pod-product-compliance
Lightning Source LLC
Chambersburg PA
CBHW032052040426
42449CB00007B/1077